I0477255

On A Sales Call

Mike Smart

ISBN:
978-1503075344

DEDICATION

This book is dedicated to all the sales professionals, prospects and customers that I have had the privilege of working alongside. Thanks for your help, advice and making getting up in the morning to go to work, so much fun and rewarding in equal measure.

CONTENTS

ABOUT THE AUTHOR

- Over thirty years of selling experience, during which time I have sold, in the aggregate, contracts worth hundreds of millions of pounds;
- Earned millions of pounds in commissions and bonuses;
- Cold-called and built businesses from the ground up;
- Hired, fired, coached and ran multi-national sales teams;
- Presented to thousands of people;
- Raised millions of pounds of funding, led a flotation process;
- Bought, integrated, restructured and sold businesses; and
- Hit quota more times than failed.

I wouldn't be so arrogant as to suggest that I am, or ever have been, the best salesman in the world. I do, however, make claim to have been privileged to work with some of the best sales executives and professional buyers in industry, and have learned my craft along the way.

I could have written a thousand pages, but that would defeat the object of this book. Pick it up, read it, put it down, and then come back to it from time to time – if it makes you think about what you do, then it has added value to you as an individual, and that is good enough.

FOREWORD

"From the moment I picked up your book until I laid it down, I was convulsed with laughter.

Someday, I intend reading it."

Groucho Marx

This short book has been written to address a specific audience. Namely: You!

To keep the list brief, if you have a pulse and want to improve your communication skills, along with your general quality of life from a financial perspective, then I would recommend that you continue reading.

Running your own business or considering setting one up? This book will help you grow a business, make sure that you get the most from your sales executives and avoid missing those opportunities that are all around us.

If you are a seasoned sales professional you've probably forgotten more than you can remember. This isn't about teaching old dogs new tricks. Firstly, being good in sales is not about trickery, and secondly, one can, however old, learn new skills, and refresh those long forgot. For the long-time pro salesman, this book is about remembering about what used to make you the top of your game, and techniques that have, with age and complacency, possibly been forgotten.

As a senior business executive you may not carry a personal sales quota; shame on you. But you do have the responsibility to deliver numbers to the business. You need to be able to communicate with your customers and your employees. This book will help you in both regards, plus will make you think about stepping up and putting your head above the parapet by taking a personal target.

For those of you that trot off to work and suffer that horrible daily commute to go and do a job you hate, hopefully, this book might engender a bit of "get-up-and go." You have no one but yourself to blame if you are stuck in a rut, bored out of your mind, and going nowhere fast. Why do salespeople tend to get rewarded better than the average employee? Because they make things happen; if you don't make things happen, then no one is likely to notice you, are they?

For those of you that are housewives or house husbands, this book will provide an insight into the trials and tribulations of the person that you live with. In addition, once you have read this short book, as I am conscious that my readers have better things to do, you will have learned some new skills, which, I trust, will help in your day to day life.

On the other hand, if you are perfect in every regard, and have no need of any help or support, then please go about your daily routine none the wiser about what this book may or may not contain. You probably fall into the unconsciously competent or unconsciously incompetent quadrants - see p145.

It would be fascinating to know how many people simply skipped, at this juncture, to page 145........

So, dear reader, either you have stayed with me or gone to page 145, realised it's not there (subject of another book....) and returned to continue on our journey.

Some ground rules before we get going.

Rule 1: I've not put a lot of prose in this book. I've written a number of thrillers, and I, along with my readership, like books to be short on flowery nonsense, but long on action. You can buy them at Amazon – The Max Thatcher Series, by Mike Smart, or visit my web site www.mikesmartauthor.co.uk. This book has been written in a similar vein.

Rule 2: I could start every chapter or thought process with some obsequious and banal comment about "in my humble opinion", or "respectfully this or that". That's simply not going to happen. It would take up far too much of your reading time, and, frankly, I'm giving you some advice based on thirty years of successful commercial selling. It's up to you to digest, come to your own conclusions about what works in your environment, and what YOU as an individual are happy to work with.

Rule 3: Please accept that his/her product/service are both interchangeable.

Rule 4: If you're looking for magic "silver bullets" that will suddenly propel you to fame and fortune, then you're looking in the wrong place. Buy a lottery ticket instead. I hate to rain on your parade, but the reality is that unless you are very fortunate, one tends to get back what one puts into life. If you put no effort in to improving your skills, if you sit on your backside and don't go out and meet people, if you are happy always coming second, then, guess what…..there ain't going to be a lot of change in your circumstances.

The book has been divided into days of the week – not because you can only do things on a certain day, but to encourage you to think about selling as a process.

MONDAY - PREPARATION

"We become what we think about." – Earl Nightingale

Topics we're going to consider:

- Are sales people born or are they made?
- Mental attitude;
- Learning and listening;
- Understanding the process;
- What are we selling?
- Understanding our product or service;
- Features versus benefits; and
- Competitive analysis.

Are sales people born or are they made?

How many times has one heard "He/She is a natural salesman"? I'm going to guess more than once……… The reality is that we are all born sales people; children are brilliant salesmen. They are relentless in pursuit of a deal:

Fig. 1

"Daddy/Mummy please (ok, so not all kids use please) can I have an ice cream?" A legitimate request made countless times at home, on holiday or wherever.

"No" A pretty standard response.

"Why?" Great killer question. Why, is a hard question, and has to be used carefully, as, potentially, sometimes comes across as being aggressive, particularly between adults. I've made my mind up, so why the question? From a child, it's an honest request for clarification.

"You've just had lunch". Call that an explanation? Sounds more like a false objection, and typically doesn't resonate, as the kid still wants their ice cream…

"Ok, so that means we've agreed, I can have one, and that it's only an issue of timing." My language, not that of a child, but the point is clear.

Fig. 2

"Daddy can I have new football?"

"No"

"But little Bertie next door has one". Fabulous emotional blackmail, and also establishes that the original request wasn't daft.

"You can't, because you lost the last one" A sensible reason, but how relevant? Balls and fences equals occupational hazard.

"I won't play near the fence". Top-class objection handling, and comes naturally. Kids understand the problem; here's the solution.

"The answer is still no!" Mmm.. the child has offered to fix the problem. Are there other conditions?

"Why?" I've addressed your concern to the best of my ability.

"I've told you". No you haven't, you're simply restating your first answer.

"That's not fair - what if I promise not lose this one?" So we have emotional blackmail now in spades. It's not fair, because the neighbour has one, and the parent, if continues by refusing the perfectly reasonable request, backed up with a promise, is illustrating a total lack of trust in their son/daughter.

Children are relentless in their pursuit of what they want. They simply will not take no for an answer, and will badger away until they invariably get what they want. They have no concept of whether what they ask for is entirely reasonable; they just know what they want, and go for it.

There are clearly correlations between gene pools and one's ability to excel at certain physical activities. Despite how hard I might train, I'm never going to be able to beat a top-class athlete like Usain Bolt; I have short legs for my 6ft 2 frame. The fact I like cigars, wine and good food probably doesn't help! However, on the flip side, I don't believe for one moment that he could not be a match for me in sales.

From the moment we are born, we sell. We are, however, products of our environment, and over time, our willingness to keep asking those awkward questions is knocked out of us. Shyness is not a trait that we are inhibited by when we are young children. It's only the pictures of us naked or in nappies on the beach when we were toddlers that appear at our 21st birthday or wedding that cause a degree of mock embarrassment. We are, indeed, all born equal. Our upbringings, our education and the circle of friends that one's parents mix with, determine whether one's sales skills continue to be enhanced, or are squeezed out of you.

We used to be fearless about asking for something, i.e. an order. As we get older, we are far less likely to push for something, and we hate running the gauntlet of being rejected. So I don't believe for one moment that sales people are born - we are all capable of being excellent sales professionals. We simply have to remember what we once did naturally.

Mental Attitude

In our youth we were fearless. In our youth we believed that we would live forever, or we would go out in a ball of flame, rather than simply fade away – yes, the more musically inclined among you will recognise there is a song in there….

Being any good in sales, starts with a basic level of self-belief. This is followed by an honest belief in one's product or services. If you don't have confidence in yourself or your product, why on earth would anybody else, and why, therefore would they want to do business with you? This is not simply about selling products, it's about selling oneself – and here's the point boys and girls: in every-day life we are selling ourselves all the time.

We are all human beings. An extreme example; manic depression is a very unfortunate condition, and I don't seek to make fun, but simply point out that I don't know many people that would, out of choice, surround themselves with manic depressives. I'm not suggesting for one moment that you are a latent manic depressive, hopefully far from it, but I am trying to make you think about your attitude to life and how you portray yourself in your home, social and work environments. Good sales people work hard at trying to get a good balance of being upbeat and positive with being pragmatic, and sensible about what's going on around them. They clearly believe in themselves and their products, and go to great lengths to ensure their prospective customers appreciate this, and begin to share their enthusiasm for the product being sold.

Now, this doesn't mean that every time you walk into a room that you run around and give high fives to all and sundry, but neither does it mean that you should be happy sitting in the back of a room or at dinner party contributing nothing. You have your opinions, you have your belief structure, and you are entitled to share them. Not everyone will agree with you, then neither would you agree necessarily with what other people have to say, but all have the right to stand up for what they believe in. Sales is no black art, it's about conveying your honest beliefs to another individual in such a way as not to cause offence, but so that people sit up and take notice.

So be positive about yourself and what you believe in; people can smell and sense insecurity and falseness a mile off. You do, so why would anybody that you interact with, be any different?

Listening And Learning

If you are talking you are not listening. There's a time to speak, and there's a time to hold one's peace and listen to what's being said. There is a real art to listening: it's called keeping your mouth shut. It never ceases to amaze me how difficult people find this to do. I've been on a number of sales calls with senior, or more junior sales resources, who just can't stop themselves. And yes, I've even managed to fall into the trap of liking to hear the sound of my own voice, more than that of the person I'm with.

In social networks, those people who talk a lot and never listen, are typically referred to as "bores" in the commercial world; they are frequently called "unemployed". We'll come on to more subtle techniques later in the book, but this very basic skill has to be learned from the get go. On the one side, it is a truism that people do like the sound of their own voice and do not appreciate being talked over. If they're a prospect or a social acquaintance, they may well be trying to impart really useful information that will help you get what you want.

Making statements and delivering long oratories on a particular subject, will, as a rule, not endear you to anyone. Standing up at a conference, delivering a presentation, or making a speech at a wedding, is one thing. Sitting in a meeting, or talking with someone at a social gathering, is quite another. There are two strands of thought that I would like to get you to think about:

Firstly, always try and use open questions early in a conversation. Who, what, where, when, how…..? Let the person speak, don't jump in at the first opportunity to correct them, or try and convince them that you have a more valid point of view. Your time, trust me, will come. As an aside, back in the good old days when taking people out for a bit of corporate hospitality wasn't considered a bribe, I always found that taking a customer or prospective to a cricket match, was a brilliant way of building a relationship, and finding out what was going on in an account.

The great temptation when you've got Mr or Mrs Smith, your most important prospect/customer out for the day, is to start selling from the moment you get them in your sights. Big mistake, they're half expecting this, and much like you or I, would actually prefer to have a nice day out on *their* terms and get to know you gradually. A cricket match is brilliant, leave them alone, make polite conversation, and if you know a little about the sport, perhaps share some interesting facts. A couple of hours in, people begin to relax; they will come to you and initiate a conversation – the pace of a cricket match is such that, invariably, there are great expanses of time with not much going on. Well guess what, after a while, any normal person actually wants to start filling these gaps, and hey presto, you get what you want on *your* terms. Golf is good too in this regard; football and theatre less so, because they're over more quickly, and trying to sell something whilst watching *Les Miserables,* is downright tricky.

We do, however, want to make sure that when we say something it has weight, and demonstrates that we are worthy of our companions time. I don't care if it's in a business or social environment, try and add value to a conversation rather than say nothing, or worse, say something stupid. There is no shame in not being able to contribute to a discussion about nuclear fusion, if this not your chosen specialist subject. You might learn something by listening, and believe it or not, even in this extreme example, by listening, one might pick up elements which you can re-use to your advantage later.

If we speak, we do so to add value, to demonstrate that we know about the subject matter, and that we are also clearly demonstrating that we are either following or guiding a discussion path. We listen hard because we want to learn, to pay respect to the person speaking, and to be able to assimilate information which we can use later.

Me, My Products, And What's The Competition Doing?

Before we hit the road and go out and meet our prospective customers, we need to make sure that we really understand our product. An obvious statement? Good, then you'd probably be staggered to know how many people simply wander out of the front door, not having done any basic research. How few really get under the covers and understood the workings of their offering, nor taken the time to understand how it compares with what's already in the market.

If you don't understand the strengths and weaknesses of your product, then you are going to fail in the big bad world of reality. You need to lead people to your strengths, and away from your weaknesses; you need to know how your product can help, and provide real examples. Your weaknesses, (and there will always be some), need to be balanced against strengths, and questioning whether the gaps in your armoury are really material to what a prospective customer might be looking for. No one is perfect, nor are their products. Avoid a negative sell, but if you know what your competitions weaknesses are, then there is no harm in stressing your strengths, if they happen to be in the areas where your competitors are weak.

Be realistic - unique is a big word, and should be used sparingly. The world is a big place, and the likelihood that your product has unique function, is, in truth, pretty remote – that's not a problem, it's a fact. What should be unique, is how you combine the features of your product within an overall package. No one else can replicate you, your company ethos, your intellect, and your desire to provide a good service.

Understand the differences between features and benefits. "This car can go from zero to a hundred and fifty miles an hour in less than six seconds". This is a feature. The benefit is that doing this on a public road, will mean that you'll only have to do it once before you lose your licence. Ok, so it's a questionable benefit, but you get the message. So when you are thinking about how to position your product, or indeed yourself, try and work out half a dozen features, and then what the linking benefits are.

As you become more proficient with your technique, you will be able to avoid simply rolling out features and benefits as part of a standard pitch. So, instead of propounding features, and then explaining the benefits, try doing it the other way around. "So, Mr Customer, if you want to lose your licence in one go, then have I got the product for you!"

Selling is not trickery, but good selling does rely on technique. Not surprisingly, the more one practices, the better one becomes. It should become second nature to be able to roll out a mixture of features and benefits in such a way that it becomes part of a conversation. The next time you meet someone for the first time, try to incorporate features and benefits of you, the person. You will do some of this already, but try adding some structure, and know that you are doing it. You may be surprised by the results.

Understanding The Process

Think people buy things almost by accident? Nope, let me try and dispel that particular myth; I would be hard pushed to think of any purchase that I've made recently which has not had some form of marketing or sales process attached. This book doesn't attempt to go into marketing in any great detail, but I would simply illustrate the point about how purchases are made, by using the example of a supermarket. From the time you walk into a store to buy a tin of something, you are being controlled. These guys spend inordinate amounts of money on deciding what they put where on display, the height on the shelf, the location in relation to other products, the special price promotions; everything is worked out to the $n'th$ degree. It's really no surprise that you end up invariably coming out of the store with more than just the tin you went in for.

We have all been sold to, and marketed at, by these huge businesses - it's not normally a random selection when you go out and buy something.

When you are out there selling, you have to understand that there is a process, a lifecycle if you will, to a sales campaign. Depending on what one is selling, the process might last only a few hours, or it could take years to come to fruition. Those of us that have worked in high value multi-million pound contracts have to continually remind ourselves of the necessity to remain patient. One slip, one badly constructed letter and an offhand comment misconstrued, and months, if not years, of work could be wasted.

We need to begin as we have with understanding who we are, and remembering that we need to be confident, and that we should be listening more than we are talking. We need to understand our product and where it fits in our customer's world, and once we've done these very basic things, we can then contemplate getting stuck into our first sales cycle. We're going to do some prospecting, some presentations, undertake qualification (a process which happens all the time), close a deal, and negotiate the terms.

The major steps in the sales process are:

- **Preparation;**

- **Generating a pipeline;**

- **On a sales call;**

- **The sales pursuit; and**

- **Closing.**

TUESDAY – GENERATING A PIPELINE

'Dry lines catch nay fish" – Salmon Fishing Expression

Let's get a couple a basics out on the table. Without a pipeline, we have nothing.   We've done our preparation, we're mentally prepared, we understand our product, and have a decent appreciation of what we are competing with. We need to feed a hopper with prospects - we will manage these prospects through a sales cycle, some of which will be discarded *en-route*, and those that remain, we will close, and they will ultimately become our valued customer.

Identifying Our Target Customers

If we take what we know about our products from a features and benefits perspective, we should be able to define those businesses or individuals that are most likely to have an interest in our offerings. Well that's done then………….

Depending on what you are selling, your prospect list could run into the millions, or perhaps at the other extreme, only be a handful of names worldwide. The prospective target market for packets of crisps is significantly larger than multi-million pound motor yachts. Well, let's "qualify that". Millions of people would like to buy a floating gin palace, but few can afford to fill up the diesel tanks, let alone afford to run one for a season.

The point here, is to be realistic about who is ultimately really going to turn into a customer; there is no point chasing everyone. I've seen it any number of times in my career where sales people have trooped off to see a customer, who, for the sake of an example, is an Oracle development shop. The sales executive in question is selling DB2 – to those of you that are non-technical, this is the equivalent of selling round pegs to someone who believes that all holes should be square.

If one has no one else to talk to, then, unfortunately, the reality is, that one does have to go and talk to those prospects who are, frankly, less than likely to turn into a customer. There is always the element of "nothing ventured nothing gained". However, the key issue is to ensure that one is focusing one's primary efforts on those whom you are, most likely, to reach an agreement with.

Qualification is a key activity throughout the sales process. It starts now, i.e. at the prospecting stage, and will continue throughout the whole life cycle of the engagement. There is no point in having a prospect list that is incredibly long, if, in reality, no one on the list is going to buy the product. It has also been a source of irritation when I've run sales teams, to have to explain the difference between being busy and being productive. Yes, one could spend each and every day in meetings from dawn until dusk, but if you are in the wrong meetings, they are a pointless exercise. I spend a significant amount of time thinking about what I'm doing - my time is valuable and finite. Why waste it?

In our personal lives we naturally tend to associate with people with whom we have common interests, and whose company that we enjoy. In simple terms, this is a classic example of how very close and complex relationships are built, without people actually giving it much thought. We don't tend to sit at home and plan whom we would like to go out and meet for an evening. We might decide that we are going to a particular type of music concert or sporting event, and, by default, we will, most likely, find people with whom we share a common interest. A bond is built, and a relationship may well ensue.

When we go through and begin to build a prospect list, the first stage in building a sales pipeline, we need to be cognizant of what we have in the kit bag, and seek to match that with what our prospective customer might be looking for. The list has to be realistic; a mixture of whether our product fits a probable requirement and can be delivered at a price point that a customer can afford. In our social engagements, it's not measured in financial terms, but rather whether there is a good fit in terms of respective personalities and a commonality, as regards people's more aspirational objectives.

Reaching Out

When I started selling all those years ago, I went out and cold called. My first commercial sales job involved selling computer stationery, more precisely, forms for printers i.e. invoices, pay slips, remittance advices etc. My target market was huge, my territory was W1 and W2 in central London. Two great post codes for a young enthusiastic eighteen year old. I'd been on a sales training day; run by a small company, backed up by highly entertaining videos from Video Arts Limited - all staring John Cleese. I had been taught about the process of creating printed continuous forms by my employer, and left in no doubt that my product was the best in the market, and that everyone would be really pleased to see me turn up at their doorstep.

The truth was something of a disappointment. No one had told me about the competition and how busy people didn't get excited about getting unsolicited sales calls from an eighteen year-old paper salesmen. I learnt so much in the six months that I did this really tough job; the lessons have stayed with me forever. Most of my thirty years plus in sales have been spent selling high value, seven figure-plus contracts – the underlying process to securing a £500 order for paper, and a £60m outsourcing contract, are, however, fundamentally the same.

Finding prospects to fill the top half of the sales funnel follows exactly the same process, though some of the tools have changed.

Cold calling

Today it's much harder to walk the streets of a city and get in the door to meet a prospective customer. Wandering in off the street uninvited and asking the receptionist if the CEO of a FTSE 100 is available for a quick chat, is unlikely to produce much of a result. It wouldn't have been much different thirty years ago. Today's equivalent of cold calling is typically confined to making phone calls. Getting past "gatekeepers" in the shape of PA's is very hard; indeed, in many cases, those people that are the target of a lot of unsolicited cold calls, simply go entirely off radar.

The key issue is to make sure that one works out early on who is the person, or more likely persons, within an organisation that are the most appropriate contacts to speak with. Almost all decisions of any magnitude are made by committee, there will be leaders in a business that drive decisions (Decision Makers), but invariably, these individuals will look to other members of the organisation for their endorsement (Influencers).

Once upon a time sales activities used to be almost

entirely driven in the direction of establishing who was the budget holder, and focusing one's efforts on convincing them. In my opinion, this was, and experience has taught me, a mistake. Buying things on behalf of an organisation has a degree of risk associated with it. It's human nature to look to, in effect, share the risk, to share the potential of making a bad decision, by looking to other people around you for a nod, or some form of affirmation that you are not doing something daft.

In our social lives, this happens all the time; we intuitively may well like someone, but can't resist checking with a close confidant, "So what do you think of so and so?" Similarly, we like to confirm with our friends what they might have heard back from a prospective friend about us – so why would it work any different in the commercial world? Clearly, it doesn't. It is entirely human nature.

Social Media

To my mind, social media, and in particular the usage of sites such as Linked-In as a means of reaching a prospective target customer, is now very passé. It's too easy to send a message to an individual. What's wrong with that? Well the truth is that everyone does it, and we're back to square one – our prospect is inundated with hundreds of requests daily/weekly for their time. How do you feel about unsolicited phone calls or bland emails? Same difference. You are a sales executive, but you are also a prospective customer for someone else; ask yourself how would you like to be approached?

Completely ignore? No. Social media sites have a role to play. However, to rely on them would be a mistake. If anything, I believe they are helpful in providing background material - some of the detail posted is even accurate.

Email/Letter

I rarely, if ever, now send a letter to a prospective business customer via the postal system. I will write a letter and post it to say thank you to a personal friend, or if I want to express condolences for a family bereavement.

I will write a letter in the form of an email to a target customer, and, depending on how concise and pertinent one makes this, one can achieve good results. Historically, a return of 1%-2% would be expected for a blanket mailshot. Depending on your product, this might well generate a decent pipeline. In high value deals this won't; simply because the target market is that much smaller.

A good, focused letter sent via an email and not structured as a bland mailshot i.e. it's personalised by name, by company, and the content is very focused, will return 15%-30%; a much more sensible response. It requires one to think about what one writes, and ensure that the content catches the reader's imagination immediately.

A combination of a good introductory letter, followed up by a call, would be my preference. It gives you a legitimate reason to phone the prospect, and a "gatekeeper" has less opportunity to prevent you getting through. A good PA is there to look after his/her boss; it's not to prevent new ideas being presented, or to inhibit the beginning of a dialogue. You have to be careful - there is a fine line between being insistent about speaking to someone and being rude (which is inexcusable). If your letter is "punchy" and has merit, you will get a response.

Targeted Meeting In Person

A good way to meet people is to go to places that they also go to. If you know who you want to meet, consider where they might go: a seminar? a training course? a certain type of recreation? This approach requires a degree of research, and an acceptance that you will have to make the effort to cross the line into someone's personal space and introduce oneself. Sounds simple? It is, but a lot of people don't have the confidence to stop someone at a conference and introduce oneself.

If you are going to be successful in sales, then you will need to be confident in yourself and in the product you have to sell. Done politely, no one has a problem with someone introducing themselves and asking for the opportunity to discuss a proposition for a couple of minutes. This used to be referred to as the elevator pitch, i.e. the person you've been trying to contact for months suddenly appears in a lift with you, and you have ninety seconds to get their attention. Well, in my experience, that rarely happens, and more often than not, there is someone else in the lift, which rather cramps your style……

Don't stalk people. Wait for a moment when the person you would like to meet has finished a conversation, or does not appear to be engrossed in something else. Accosting people in the toilet is not going to endear you…..be polite, explain who you are, and ask for a couple of minutes of their time. Most, not all, people will be polite and give you time of day – it's human nature…..how the conversation develops will depend on whether what you have to offer sparks an interest.

Make Yourself Interesting

The speakers at a conference, seminar or training course have a great opportunity to sell not only their company's wares, but equally important, themselves. An audience does not want to sit there and be "pitched" to, they are there to learn, and will gauge the product; not only as much on the long list of features and benefits poured out, but also the quality and style of the delivery. We'll come back to this, but if you want to meet people, make sure that you are someone that *they* want to meet. This can be achieved by putting yourself in the limelight i.e. public event, or, alternatively, try writing and publishing thought-provoking issues through some form of PR.

One can easily relate this to more social engagements. At a dinner party, someone who has interesting opinions and expresses these, will, invariably, be engaged in discussion by other people. Some may or may not be close acquaintances. In my experience, most first meetings between new couples are arranged by the wife or partner. This is not sexist, it's simply that they tend to meet other wives and mums at school gates, and develop a social relationship which leads to a "we ought to arrange to go out for a drink, or have dinner." It's only at this juncture that the husbands meet, the ongoing strength and depth of ongoing relationships are normally determined at this point. All parties need to get on, and how well you get on, will be determined by the social interaction - and we are all intentionally, or sub consciously, selling ourselves during this process.

As an observation, in my experience, few social relationships, developed through a work environment tend to blossom into family wide affair. One needs to be extremely careful not to overstep the mark. Individuals like a separation between work and play.

Demand Pull

This is also a function of making oneself interesting. A simplistic example would be those people that are very much in the public gaze i.e. actors, musicians and sportsman. We, in the general populace, are attracted to their fame; they are, after all perceived as being interesting...

Many of you will have the benefit of marketing departments; their role is to help generate interest and footfall. From a sales perspective, it's obviously attractive to be able to engage with people that have expressed an interest in your product.

As a sales executive or business owner, you can create demand pull through using your existing accounts, to generate referral sales. Leads from happy customers are fantastic; the reality is, though, one has to ask, and not rely on them doing the opening sales call for you......

WEDNESDAY – ON A SALES CALL

"You can never cross the ocean until you have the courage to lose sight of the shore." – Christopher Columbus

People buy people

Many of us who have worked as sales professionals for several years have attended multi-day seminars, and been encouraged to read tomes of books that break down the selling process into a myriad of steps. This book/ guide, call it what you will, has been designed to simplify the process. It will hopefully provoke as many questions as it will answers. That's goodness in my opinion. It will make you question what you do, how you interact, and how you go out and sell yourself and your company's products.

There are lots of clever, highly analytical books in the market. There are very expensive courses you can, and perhaps should consider attending, to improve your skills. But there is one inalienable FACT that one needs to grasp, and can be passed on here at limited expense: People buy People, and EVERYONE IS DIFFERENT.

We can't change who we are; we can manage our persona, and we can control how we interrelate with people, and we need to change our style and approach to match what is sitting opposite us.

There is plenty of material available about communication styles and personality types. These can be studied further through systems such as Myers-Briggs and Carl Jung, but for our purposes, there are four main 'types' of people, and recognising this and communicating in the most effective way for that 'type', will serve you well.

In your sales process you may encounter those people who love detail. They are very structured and well-organised - thriving on data and focus. In order to successfully engage with people who display these traits, demonstrate your product knowledge. Support your statements with proof, and don't rush them. Remain formal in your communications, and when handling their objections, ask searching questions.

You will, without doubt, meet those who are extrovert, sociable and love entertaining and being entertained.

They like to talk about themselves, so let them! Show interest in them, offer incentives and deals. These people love stories, don't like too much detail, and are always interested in what's next, so focus on the future and further benefits to come.

Our third 'type' is the more introverted, 'feeling' person who is concerned with harmony, agreement and consensus. They need time to reflect, and come across as relaxed, informal and people-focused. When communicating with them, be open, speak slowly, show you care, listen well, and seek their feedback. Explain the benefits of your product or service, particularly the people benefits, and don't push them if they have objections.

The decision makers in many of the sales situations you encounter, may well be the fourth 'type'. These are often the senior leaders who are busy, efficient, formal, and want the information delivered in a direct, concise manner. They deal in facts, so be well organised, well-prepared, and don't waffle. Watch out for them to become impatient, use reflective questions to handle their objections, and clearly state alternatives.

No-one is purely one 'type'; we all have some of each trait. Recognising the preferences of the people you are dealing with, means you can adapt your communication style accordingly, and build more effective relationships.

Dress to at least a standard that you believe your prospect would expect; it's a judgement call. For the most part, it's best to "over dress" - you'll create less offence. Don't be late. It may be fashionable to be late for a dinner party, but it's downright rude to keep a prospective customer waiting. Personally, I don't believe it's acceptable to keep anybody waiting; there's no good reason other than you didn't allow enough time to reach your destination. If you are going to be late, then let whomever is waiting for you know. It's not hard, and as is a common courtesy.

Every business meeting and every social engagement that one attends is fundamentally a sales call of some description. If you wander into an internal meeting or a regular customer meeting unprepared, you are not doing your job properly. You should be clear about what the purpose of the meeting is, why are you there, and what outcome/s you are seeking from the meeting.

It staggers me how many people don't have this basic structure in mind, and probably explains why so many meetings, internally or externally, simply end up as a nice chat. A customer's time is valuable, as is yours. Why waste it? We've worked hard to earn the right to have the meeting in the first place - why on earth would I now want to leave with nothing to show for it? Why would the prospective customer be happy to once again open their diary, if they come away with nothing of merit. Executives in business understand intuitively why you are sitting in their office; they are not daft.

After the opening pleasantries:

- Set out who you are, what your background is, so as to establish some credibility, and what it is that you would like to discuss.
- Ask (politely) open questions about the person sitting opposite you:
    - Have they been with the business long?
    - What are their (commercial) issues and priorities?
    - Seek to confirm what you may have gleaned from your profiling of the individual and market research on the business.
- Listen more than speak.
- Once you have a good appreciation of your audience and what they might be interested in, ask for permission to explain what it is that you have to offer.
    - Encourage questions.
    - Stop and check that a specific point has been understood.
    - Look for indications that what you are saying is of interest.
        - What's the body language like, is the audience asleep or sitting forward and making notes?
        - Are you getting any probing questions, seeking out more detail; a good sign!
- Work on these questions, find out why they are important.

- Offer new ideas and seek to add value
    - You will visit a lot of prospects in your career - you will see a lot of common problems. Use your intellect and imagination to suggest new concepts and approaches which may not have been considered
- Remember that you know your product and presentation - your audience doesn't.
    - Take time to explain, but do not bore to tears.

Presentation

A lot of people use PowerPoint, or something similar. It's a great tool, very graphical (in the hands of the right designer), or can become a boring set of bullet points read off in sequence by the presenter. If you know your material, you should not need to look at the screen. You have rehearsed this presentation a hundred times in your mind before you delivered it. Oh, you put it together on the train before you arrived. Mmm…not ideal.

If you run through the presentation, and you role-play the meeting in your mind several times beforehand, it is most likely that you will not be caught off guard. You will already have worked out answers for the majority of questions, and you will create an aura of confidence. And always remember that the buyer wants to be confident in his prospective supplier, and it all starts with the first sales presentation.

For many presentations which are only to one or two people, I prefer to "turn pages" across a desk or boardroom table. My presentation material will be printed off, I give the option of delivering a PowerPoint or simply going through "together", in a collaborative style - a series of slides. My slides will normally only have a few bullet points on each, I (this means YOU),the presenter, add the value, and not reliant on snazzy graphics to convey my expertise in the specific market, nor deep understanding of my product.

People buy people. You have to be able to demonstrate an understanding of what a prospective customer is looking for. You need to relate your product to these needs. You should not assume that you know what the customer wants, but have asked before beginning the presentation, so you can draw out the elements. You should know your presentation forwards/backwards and sideways, this will allow you to move easily through sections which you now know will be of limited interest, whilst focusing on those that are really important.

By the end of the first sales call, we should have met some, if not all, of our objectives.

These will include:

- Developing a personal rapport with the prospect. Hopefully, we might have found some common non work-related areas of interest.

ON A SALES CALL

- We will come away with a decent understanding of what our prospect does within the organisation, and where he/she sits in the overall business.
- We will have a good understanding of what might be the pressing business issues of the day.
- We will have begun to explain how what we have to offer, will help address their problems.
- During our meeting, we have asked questions relating to size of budget. What is the timing of making a decision?
- What is the internal process, who else might be involved, is it a competitive bid process?
- We will have confirmed whether what we have presented/discussed is of interest, are there any glaring gaps in our proposal? Are there any major concerns?
- We will come away with an agreed action plan of next steps, which will include a date for a further meeting, or at least a confirmation that the prospect is happy to engage again as appropriate.

A new business sales cycle, depending on product will comprise any number of meetings, telephone calls and correspondence. Some products can be sold at a single meeting, others might take years – it doesn't matter; the recognition of the process and strict discipline has to be there every time. As sales people become more experienced, they tend to forget these basic rules. New sales people are typically uncomfortable with the approach, because it's not a set of skills which they have fully mastered.

REMEMBER:

You must rehearse and role play;

You must do your homework;

You should have clear objectives in mind; and

You should let the prospect/customer speak.

Listen really hard, ask sensible, open questions, and then use the responses when you present, to demonstrate that you were listening, and are not simply delivering an "out-of-the-can" presentation.

You should present in such a way as to inform, but not to bore.

Throughout a one-on-one meeting, seek to confirm That what you are saying is of interest.

You should add value to your material; a buyer isn't buying PowerPoint, he's buying you!

There has to be an agreed set of next steps. Sometimes these will be major in nature, and other times they will be trivial, but in all cases, you will have secured the opportunity of re-engaging.

Don't forget to thank the prospect/customer/audience for their time, both at the start and at the end of the meeting/presentation.

THURSDAY – THE SALES PURSUIT

"Never give up, never surrender!" A great line from Galaxy Quest, an excellent spoof of Star Trek.

We've had a couple of sales calls; we know there is a requirement, and we're in a competitive environment.

Key Pointers:

- In all probability, there is more than one person involved in the buying cycle.
    - Are you spending your time with the right people?

The temptation is always to stick talking with the people that you like, and the ones that you think like you. Sometimes, these are indeed the right individuals to spend your time with. Unfortunately, in many cases, they may not be, and whilst they are really nice to you, they are equally friendly with the competition. They are human beings, and perfectly entitled to have friendships across the board; why would they only be courteous and pleasant with you?

One can learn a lot from talking with people who may not be your fan. How much influence do they wield? Are their concerns valid?

Make sure you keep a dialogue going with as many people as possible. Not only will you get a more rounded picture, but you will avoid the possibility of alienating an individual. Don't risk being labelled as a snob; it's all well and lovely talking to the CEO all day, but his direct reports will become pretty fed up if they believe that you do not value their input.

- Do you realistically have a chance of winning?
  - One has to be single-minded in pursuit of a new deal.

I remember doing a deal with a customer, where the Chairman had written a personal letter to me part way through the sales cycle, advising me that "over his dead body" would they ever do a deal. I stuck to my guns and eventually managed to get him to change his position, and see the merit in what I was proposing. Sometimes however one has to take stock and look in the proverbial mirror, and decide whether one's efforts ought to be spent elsewhere.

- Managing the tempo of a sales campaign
  - Don't become a scratched record

There is a natural lifecycle to a sales process, and try as we might, it is more likely than not that we, as sales people, can do little to influence when a particular decision falls. Offering special deals for quarter end decisions does work in some cases - normally around existing relationships, where a customer will often try to help you make a specific target. In new business this is a very risky strategy, because try as you might, once you offered an incentive, it will still be on the table from a customer perspective, even if the date is in the past.

As the sales cycle extends, it becomes increasingly hard to come up with new things to talk about, and to keep the dialogue fresh. This is a great risk to a successful completion. If one is seen to chase too much, then our prospect can become bored, and/or feel harassed. Avoid the temptation to be on the individual's case all the time. Trust me, if there is an internal process, you're not helping yourself. Of course if you get wind of a sales cycle that's already underway, but that you are late on the scene, the opposite is true. No, that doesn't mean camping on the doorstep and making a nuisance of yourself, but it does mean that you will be "new news". You will be able to ask for an explanation of what the gaps are in current proposals. I've seen it many times - the person who opens the door initially, frequently doesn't win the deal, but sets up the structure for a latecomer to walk in and secure the business.

- Your job is to confirm that the process is on track;
- To ensure that you have provided all the requisite information;
- Keep out new entrants. or at least find out if new players have entered the fray;
- Spend time with those contacts with whom you may not have a strong relationship;
- Demonstrate a mature degree of patience and appreciation for the inner workings of a business; and
- Bring in new members of your team where appropriate:
    o Build more bridges;
    o Get new perspectives.

Never Stop Qualifying The Opportunity

There are a myriad of tools and systems which one can employ to score opportunities. Many are too convoluted and too scientific for my liking. The reality is that all sales cycles are similar, and all are very different; it seems illogical to believe that one model will fit all. In my experience, prospects don't appreciate being asked "Am I going to win the deal?" every five minutes. It is, however, reasonable to ask questions about the status of your proposal. In high value transactions, the cost of bidding can run into millions of pounds, and one has to be extremely careful that good money isn't being wasted on a fruitless pursuit.

Irrespective of the size of the deal, you are spending your valuable time on a sales cycle. You owe it to yourself and your business to make sure that you have a realistic chance of being successful. In my experience, most sensible prospect/customers also understand this basic issue. You are entitled to ask open questions, you are entitled to ask for advice, and above all, you have your gut instinct to rely upon.

FRIDAY - CLOSING

"Let silence do the heavy lifting" – Susan Scott, Author "Fierce Conversations"

Are you an order taker or a salesman?

As a top-flight Sales Director I used to work for, pointed out very eloquently on any number of occasions: "It's very easy to walk down the high street, and sell £20 notes for £5".

It's simply not good enough believing that everything comes down to price. I am not so naïve as to believe that price does not play a major part in a sales/buying cycle, but if one simply sells on price alone, one is going to lose more than one wins. Furthermore, you will not be maximising the value of your product, and the benefits of dealing with your organisation.

Every product combined with you and what your

company has to offer, equates to a unique proposition. It is YOUR responsibility to weave product/you/the company together in such a way that you build differentiation into the overall proposal.

By the time we are in the short strokes of the sales cycle, your prospect should be clear about what it is that you have to offer. I appreciate that some products are more homogeneous than others; that's life. It simply means you are going to have to work harder to find those differentiation points.

A well-run sales cycle will result in a deal being closed without any big song and dance. The ideal outcome is that the prospect believes that they decided all by themselves. During my career, I've closed a lot of business - the ones that gave me the most pleasure are those where the CEO or lead buyer has gone out of their way to thank me for having done a professional job. A fellow professional respecting what you've done is a very satisfying reward.

Many times you will have to *ask* for the order, this is your job; but a huge number of people and supposed sales professional find it almost impossible to pluck up the courage to ask. Individuals hate being rejected, and of course asking the ultimate question risks it all; there is no escape, because if you don't close, someone like me is going to come into the office next and ask the prospect for the order. I'm not greatly enthused about being told "no", but I've worked out a long time ago that I need to know and that a marginal call can be won simply because I stepped across the line out of my supposed comfort zone, and asked for the order.

As a young man, I used to go out for an evening and occasionally meet attractive women. I was out prospecting; I would do my best to make myself interesting, and would make sure that I paid close attention to the person I was talking to; running a short sales cycle, and then I would close. It sounds awful; it wasn't. The only difference between me and the majority of other men and women out for a good night, is that I knew what I was doing.

There are great number of "closes", but they all break down into a few common themes which I would encourage you to learn.

The Alternative Close

"Would you like it with or without finance?" = "My place or yours?"

Here we are aiming for a prospect to make a choice, but either ends up with an order

Puppy Dog Close

"Why not try this product for a week or so?" = "Give me a go, it'll be great"

This is how photo copiers, water dispensing machines and a myriad of products are sold. Once I'm in the door, I can demonstrate how you can't live without my product. Of course the reality is we are then also relying on the fact that people are lazy, and will not then go out actively seeking alternatives. A word of caution: the close is called a puppy dog, because it also carries a risk. Puppies have a habit of chewing up shoes/furniture etc, and leaving the odd mess.

Asking for the order

"Can we go ahead on that basis?"= "Are we going to be more than friends?"

Can I have the order?

Objection handling close

If then = (could think of several unprintable examples)

We're going to cover negotiation shortly, but in this context, "If then" is the concept of offering to meet a specific objection in return for an order. i.e. "I know it's important that the widget is delivered by the end of the month. If I commit to this, may I have the order?"

The Lost Sale = "I'm devastated! I thought we were the perfect couple...perhaps you misunderstood something I did or said. Let me explain, I'm really…….."

You'd be surprised how many times one can rescue a sale at the last moment. One would use this technique when the answer given has been "No". Without becoming aggressive or indignant, and this is very important, one asks politely for an explanation. Listen very hard: has the prospect really grasped all the points of your pitch? Check back. One should always genuinely respect a prospect's decision (this is not tongue in cheek). It's true you must demonstrably respect the individual, but before you walk away, ask the question: "Had I answered that differently, would you have been happy to have gone ahead?" "Let me clarify that point as there may have been some confusion." Remember, it's your job to be clear; it's not their fault that they may have misunderstood. It's yours.........

The Negative/Aspirational Close = "I'm not sure you're the one for me......"

This is a powerful piece of reverse psychology when used correctly. Tell people they can't have something, and watch the reaction. "I'd really like to sell you this, but to be fair, I think it's little out of your reach/range." "I appreciate you would like the "go faster" stripes but that's a lot more expensive than the competition is offering - maybe in few months'/years' time..." It's turning a potential negative in your offering to a positive aspirational goal. It's human nature - many people want what they can't afford, and in a busy competitive landscape, its sometime better to put clear space between you and your competitors' offering, and, in effect, put a barrier to a buying a decision.

The "bluff" close = "I do have alternatives, you know....."

How many times have you had this pitched at you? "You need to know that there are other people looking at this car/house/holiday. If you don't buy it now, it may not be there tomorrow". In a similar vein there is the special offer/limited time period deal. Be careful, a smart buyer will call you just for fun – surprise, surprise, the deal is still there next morning/week or month....

If you use this close, be prepared to be called.

Assumptive Close = "I'm looking forward to sharing breakfast.."

This is my personal favourite, and should be used throughout a sales cycle. It can be used liberally to confirm that everything is on track. "When we do XYZ together......." "You will be a great addition to the customer base...." "I'm very pleased you've confirmed that you like our proposal......." All our phraseology, our whole demeanor is one where we have "assumed" that the deal is done, and we are simply going through a process together. I'm very well aware of the danger of making assumptions, and the making an "**ass** out of yo**u** and **me**". This close is a continuous process designed to flush out from a prospect if they have any issues. If they don't put you straight and say, "hang on a second, I never said.....", they are following your lead. Everything becomes a natural progression; try it - it works.

Selling well is a skill - something that has to be worked

on. It's not trickery, it's understanding the process. We are closing all the way through a sales cycle, trying to narrow a prospect down to the point where they agree to go ahead. Try the closes above - there are many others, but these are more likely to be variations on a theme. Try not to make it too obvious, but at some point, be prepared to take that risk, and ask for the order.

Two additional important points

Firstly, once you have asked a hard closing question please, please, SHUT UP. Don't try and help elaborate the question, put the pressure on the prospect. "Let silence do the heavy lifting."

Secondly, if you've got the order say, "Thank you", and leave. I'm not suggesting that you bolt for the door clutching your signed order, but trust me, you can only do harm by sitting there and talking more. You have nothing to gain and everything to lose. Celebratory lunch, fine, let's do it next week.

Handling Objections

It is an unfortunate reality that most prospects manage to come up with some really good objections or concerns during a sales cycle. How you go about addressing these, will determine, to a large extent, whether you end up winning the business. Please note my language; clearly, if you can answer the issues raised to someone's satisfaction, that is going to be a positive step forward, however, some points you will not be able to address fully. The WAY you answer a problem posed, is almost as important as the response itself.

In a role-play situation, one is taught to ensure that you draw out all the objections in one go, i.e. "So other than points A,B,C,D, ... are there any other reasons why you can't place an order?" This is then followed up with, "If I can address all these issues will you be placing an order?"

In the real world there are a couple of problems with this approach. Firstly, you could well end up with a page full of concerns. Think about it, you are helping crystallise a long list in the prospect's mind, and the phraseology has actually encouraged him to stop and potentially create more problems than he may well have originally considered.

Personally, I try and work on a combination of the assumptive close, described earlier, and pre-handling objections. The assumptive close will tend to draw out objections as you go through a process, in this way, as objections are flushed out, you have the opportunity to answer them and move on. If I know my product, market, competitive landscape, and, most importantly, my prospects profile, and have been listening hard, I will also have a decent appreciation of where the roadblocks might appear.

If there is a problem coming, then it is well worth considering taking it head on, early in the sales cycle, before the prospect raises the issue. "Jane, I know that you need this project delivered by the end of quarter 4, but given the requirements, that's going to be almost impossible. Is this a showstopper?" Now, you may well find it is, in which case one would then consider what could be changed in the scope of a proposal to change timelines. The prospect may well come up with some solutions of her own, a really good buying sign, as she is working with you. Alternatively, you may get something back along the lines, "Ideally, we would have it in by then, but we know that's a big ask."

The fact that you have taken the initiative, will stand you in good stead. You have demonstrated professionalism, you know where the issues lie, and once it's off the table, it's not going to come up later, and prevent an order being placed.

I'm not suggesting that you <u>look</u> for problems, but you should be mature enough to recognise where objections are likely to arise, and cover them off earlier rather than later.

When addressing concerns, you should:

- Always take them seriously, and make sure that the prospect sees that you are;
- Ask for clarification if it's not clear what's being said;
- Try and determine whether it's a real objection, (i.e. will prevent an order) or false objection (either a red herring, or something that is, in effect, a nice-to-have, and can be lived without);
- You may well have already addressed the issue in your proposal; patiently/politely point out and confirm whether this is actually the case.

- In some cases you may not be able to come up with an acceptable answer/alternative - that's life........and you will have to put this into your overall qualification process; and finally,
- NEVER LIE to fix a problem – it will come out eventually.

SATURDAY - NEGOTIATING

Groucho: "That's in every contract, that's what you call a sanity clause."

Chico: "You can't a fool a me. There ain't no sanity clause".

Negotiation is a facet of every-day life.   We negotiate with our loved ones, business partners and complete strangers all the time. The vast majority of people do so without knowing they're actually in a negotiation. Unsurprisingly, those that know what they are doing tend to end up achieving, more often than not, their desired outcomes.

One could write a whole book on the art of handling a negotiation, but in order to bulk up the content, one would, in effect, replay past experiences.   For the purposes of this guide I have broken down the process into a couple of straight-forward, more digestible elements:

The process of negotiation:

- Do unto others as you would unto yourself.
    - If you are making, in your considered opinion, unreasonable demands, how do you think the person you're negotiating with is going to view them?
- A negotiation is a two way process.
    - There will be elements in a contract or undertaking which are sacrosanct to you; find out early on where the customers "hard stops" are.
- Establish parity in the process.
    - You shouldn't bully, but neither should you allow yourself to be bullied.
    - A trained negotiator is looking for weaknesses; at certain points in the process, you should dig, and not simply roll over.
- If possible, always start with your own base contract/terms and conditions.
    - It is much easier to negotiate out elements of contract rather than to get clauses inserted.
    - Accept the premise of reciprocity.
        - What's good for you is, of course, going to be good for a buyer.
    - A contract is there for when things go wrong.

- They are an unfortunate necessity, so, have to be accepted as part of the overall process.
- A trained buyer will be wise to your sales technique; they are trained (as are you) - they will have their own techniques.
  - Look for the signs.
    - Continually reminding you that they have alternatives.
      - Really? I thought we'd just been through a process to establish the best solution for the business?
  - Respect the individual.
    - He or she will want to walk away with some demonstrable "wins". Before you go into the meeting, figure out what you can "give", but make them work for it
- "If you agree to this, then I can accommodate that" = IF …….. THEN………
  - Be careful - as noted above, a trained buyer will see an opening statement like this a mile off.
  - With a less-experienced counterpart, you can have a lot of fun with this. Try it; the main point is that you get the concession agreed before you volunteer to do anything. "If you do the washing

up and cook dinner, I'll go and cut the grass...." If you make the offer to do something in advance of getting the "give", you will be on your back foot. Get it wrong, and don't be surprised that the washing and cooking will be there when you return from grass cutting.

o The principle is to exchange items of comparable value. In a complex contract there may be 100's of these points to negotiate; on less sophisticated deals, horse trading is far easier.

- Playing poker.
  o If you are prepared to "bluff" in a contractual negotiation, be willing to get "called".
    - A trained buyer will, for the sheer hell of it, call your bluff if they think it's unwarranted, or simply a ploy
    - Once you've been caught out, your credibility, in the process, will be sharply diminished; basically, do not overplay your hand.
- Take breaks.
  o If there is a complex piece of the contract under discussion, then don't be shy about asking for a break. It's not a weakness.

- It is also a good technique if conversation is becoming overly animated, or you simply want to make a point.
  - o Never contradict one of your negotiating team in public. Take a break; sounds obvious, but have seen it many times.
- Keep your sense of humour.
  - o It's important to convey your confidence, not in an arrogant way, but so that the person across the table understands that you've been here before.
  - o A bit of lightness in the process will also help you trade off points more quickly and easily.

It's important to understand that negotiation is a key part of the sales process. In some cases, negotiation takes place before one shakes hands on a deal. On very large deals, it is customary for a decision to be made in principle before entering detailed legal discussions – the costs can be exorbitant.

Negotiating can be seen as a point-scoring competition. I would urge you to see this differently. It's an integral part of the sales process, and a skill that one needs to develop and hone. Leave the legal beagles to try and score the points from one another, your overriding concern is to manage the process, and make sure that you end up with a fair contract.

Once signed, the contract should be consigned to a filing cabinet – if it gets pulled out and poured over, then you've got a problem coming.

SUNDAY - REVIEW

"To improve is to change; to be perfect is to change often." – Winston Churchill

What's that horrible taste in my mouth? Why does my head hurt, and why am I feeling a little down this morning?

It's called a deal hangover.......

You've been out, and celebrated, quite right too, but not only are we suffering the effect of perhaps over-indulging, we are also now coming off the high of doing a deal.

When we are going through the sales cycle we are entirely wrapped up in the process, and when we win, we are on an understandable high. With the deal done we now have a void to fill; the adrenaline rush of the last few days or weeks/months has left us drained.

Today is the day we recover from our excesses, but we also use the time to reflect on how well or badly we ran the campaign.

What is it that we could have done differently?

What did we learn?

If we lost out, why?

I am firm believer that life is a journey, and that we will all enjoy ups and downs along the road. If it were always the same, where would the fun be? As professional sales people, or individuals that recognise that selling is part of day-to-day life, one has to be able to take the good and bad in our stride. What we must do is never stop learning, or, at least, keep our minds open to fresh ideas. Some will be daft, others will resonate, and you will find way of incorporating the concepts into your everyday life.

What works for one person, doesn't, by definition, necessarily work for the next. We are individuals, with our own personas, our own idiosyncrasies, and guess what? - everyone that you meet in life will have their own traits. If you believe that you can deal with everyone in the same way, then please think again – you can't, and you won't be as successful in sales, or in life generally as you could be.

I wrote this book because a number of people that I have worked with and live with, suggested that with over thirty years of experience, I might have something to offer. Well you, dear reader, will be the judge of that.

A couple of last thoughts to contemplate before we go back to work tomorrow:

We are only as good as our last sale – never stop trying to improve and achieve more.

Last week is over, good or bad, "The past is there as a reference point not a place to live in" (A modified great quote used by a friend of mine Kriss Akabusi MBE)

You can make a difference; grab the opportunity. Happy hunting and great selling!

"The only person you are destined to become is the person you decide to be." – Ralph Waldo Emerson

www.ingramcontent.com/pod-product-compliance
Lightning Source LLC
Chambersburg PA
CBHW021021180526
45163CB00005B/2056

* 9 7 8 1 5 0 3 0 7 5 3 4 4 *